My Grandpa Could do ANYTHING in THE GREAT OUTDOORS!

by Ric Dilz

Boulder, Colorado

Art & Design by Rein Designs Staff

Copyright ©2012 by Ric Dilz. All rights reserved. No part of this book may be reproduced in any form or by any electronic or mechanical means, including information storage and retrieval systems, without permission in writing from the publisher, except by a reviewer who may quote brief passages in a review.

My Grandma could do ANYTHING...

My Grandma doesn't rock climb...

But she could!

My Grandma
doesn't
fly a rescue helicopter...

But she could!

My Grandma doesn't kayak…

But she could!

My Grandma
doesn't
ski black diamonds...

But she could!

My Grandma
doesn't
lead adventure tours...

But she could!

My Grandma
doesn't
go caving...

But she could!

My Grandma
doesn't
fly fish...

But she could!

My Grandma
doesn't
hang glide...

But she could!

My Grandma
doesn't
work as a forest ranger...

But she could!

My Grandma
doesn't
ride a mountain bike...

But she could!

My Grandma
doesn't
water ski...

But she could!

My Grandma doesn't sing around the campfire...

But she could!

My Grandma
could do lots of things,
but I'm so happy with
the one thing she does
the best...

Animal Fun Facts

A bear sleeps all winter.

 Did you know he sleeps in his bear feet?

Moose can protect themselves from bug bites by dunking themselves in water.

 Do you think they need to use a snorkel?

Deer are excellent swimmers and can swim across lakes and streams.

 Would a deer do the doggy paddle?

The largest rainbow trout caught on record was 57 pounds.

 That's a whale of a trout!

A beaver's front teeth never stop growing. They keep them the perfect size by chewing on wood.

 It's like a haircut for their teeth.

Skunks can spray their stink liquid up to 10 feet!

 Let's make sure we stand at least 20 feet from a skunk!

When diving from the sky, the eagle can reach speeds up to 200 miles per hour.

 Wow, he's got a need for speed... like you.

When a rabbit is happy, it will click or grind its teeth.

 I know you're happy when you grind your teeth on a cookie.

Visit www.reindesigns.com for more fun products!

Published by Rein Designs, Inc.
Boulder, Colorado

Text and Illustration Copyright ©2012 by Ric Dilz. All rights reserved. No part of this book may be reproduced in any form or by any electronic or mechanical means, including information storage and retrieval systems, without permission in writing from the publisher, except by a reviewer who may quote brief passages in a review.

ISBN 978-0-9758704-9-5

Library of Congress Control Number: 2012905119

Printed in China